Understanding the Cultures of the Middle East

Geography, Government, and Conflict across the Middle East

Bridey Heing

Cavendish Square
New York

Published in 2017 by Cavendish Square Publishing, LLC
243 5th Avenue, Suite 136, New York, NY 10016

Copyright © 2017 by Cavendish Square Publishing, LLC

First Edition

No part of this publication may be reproduced, stored in a retrieval system, or transmitted in any form or by any means—electronic, mechanical, photocopying, recording, or otherwise—without the prior permission of the copyright owner. Request for permission should be addressed to Permissions, Cavendish Square Publishing, 243 5th Avenue, Suite 136, New York, NY 10016. Tel (877) 980-4450; fax (877) 980-4454.

Website: cavendishsq.com

This publication represents the opinions and views of the author based on his or her personal experience, knowledge, and research. The information in this book serves as a general guide only. The author and publisher have used their best efforts in preparing this book and disclaim liability rising directly or indirectly from the use and application of this book.

CPSIA Compliance Information: Batch #CW17CSQ

All websites were available and accurate when this book was sent to press.

Library of Congress Cataloging-in-Publication Data

Names: Heing, Bridey.
Title: Geography, government, and conflict across the Middle East / Bridey Heing.
Description: New York : Cavendish Square, 2017. | Series: Understanding the cultures of the Middle East| Includes index.
Identifiers: ISBN 9781502623676 (library bound) | ISBN 9781502623683 (ebook)
Subjects: LCSH: Middle East--Juvenile literature. | Middle East--Geography--Juvenile literature. | Middle East--Politics and government--1945- --Juvenile literature.
Classification: LCC DS44.H44 2017 | DDC 956--dc23

Editorial Director: David McNamara
Editor: Elizabeth Schmermund
Copy Editor: Rebecca Rohan
Associate Art Director: Amy Greenan
Senior Designer: Alan Sliwinski
Production Coordinator: Karol Szymczuk
Photo Research: J8 Media

The photographs in this book are used by permission and through the courtesy of: Cover George Steinmetz/Corbis Documentary/Getty Images; p. 4 Rickyd/Shutterstock.com; p. 7 Leemage/UIG/Getty Images; p. 10 Print Collector/Hulton Archive/Getty Images; p. 14 Orijentolog/File:Saint Sarkis Cathedral & Imam Khomeini, Tehran.jpg/Wikimedia Commons; p. 22 PhotoQuest/Archive Photos/Getty Images; p. 30 Keystone-France/Gamma Keystone/Getty Images; p. 34 Anadolu Agency/Getty Images; p. 38 Chesnot/Getty Images; p. 41 Public Domain/Crockett John/File:Assassin-Gate-Photo-by-John-W-Crockett.JPG/Wikimedia Commons; p. 47 Bahrain viewbook/File:Protests in Bahrain, February 2011 43.jpg/Wikimedia Commons; p. 50 Ali Mansuri/File:Supplicating Pilgrim at Masjid Al Haram. Mecca, Saudi Arabia.jpg/Wikipedia; p. 52 Public Domain/Teo Gomez/File:Petra Deir 44.jpg/Wikimedia Commons; p. 55 Ahmed Abd El-Fatah (http://www.flickr.com/people/30572015@N06) from Egypt/File:Tahrir Square on July 29 2011.jpg/Wikimedia Commons; p. 578 U.S. Department of State/File:Clinton Netanyahu Abbas 15 Sep 2010.jpg/Wikimedia Commons; p. 60 Raad Adayleh-Pool/Getty Images; p. 65 BENAINOUS/HOUNSFIELD/Gamma-Rapho/Getty Images; p. 69 Amine Landoulsi/Anadolu Agency/Getty Images; p. 70 Hermes Images/AGF/UIG/Getty Images; p. 73 Bechir Ramzy/Anadolu Agency/Getty Images; p. 75 U.S. Navy photo by Mass Communication Specialist 2nd Class Jesse B. Awalt/Released/File:Muammar al-Gaddafi at the AU summit.jpg/Wikimedia Commons; p. 80 Bundesministerium für Europa, Integration und Äußeres (https://www.flickr.com/people/88775815@N04)/File:Tunisian National Dialogue Quartet Visit to Vienna March 2016(24747151924).jpg/Wikimedia Commons; p. 82 European Commission DG ECHO (http://www.flickr.com/people/69583224@N05)/(7).jpg/Wikimedia Commons; p. 84 Iranian Religious Leader Press Office/Anadolu Agency/Getty Images; p. 91 Mehmet Kaman/Anadolu Agency/Getty Images; p. 93 Mikhail Svetlov/Getty Images; p. 95 EPA/European Pressphoto Agency/Alamy Stock Photo; p. 97 STR/AFP/Getty Images; p. 98 FETHI BELAID/AFP/Getty Images; p. 102-103 Cartarium/Shutterstock.com.

Printed in the United States of America

Contents

Introduction 5

1 The History of Geography, Government, and Conflict across the Middle East 11

2 Modern-Day Geography, Government, and Conflict in the Gulf 35

3 Modern-Day Geography Government, and Conflict in the Levant 53

4 Modern-Day Geography, Government, and Conflict in North Africa. 71

5 Important Figures in Geography, Government, and Conflict across the Middle East 85

Chronology 100

Map of the Region 102

Glossary 104

Further Information 106

Bibliography 108

Index 110

About the Author 112

Azadi Square is one of the most famous landmarks in Tehran, Iran's capital city.

Introduction

Few areas of the world receive as much attention as the Middle East and North Africa. Former colonies and **protectorates**, the countries of this region are culturally, religiously, and politically diverse, but are often painted with broad strokes as unstable and **authoritarian**. In truth, the politics of each country in this area are unique, although there are overarching historical themes at play. This book explores the many differences that define Middle Eastern and North African politics, as well as the ways in which they are similar and work together.

The Middle East stretches from Iran in the east to Morocco in North Africa and is made up of three smaller subregions. The Gulf, which borders the Red Sea and the Arabian Sea, includes Iran, Iraq, Saudi Arabia, United Arab Emirates, Oman, Yemen, Qatar, Bahrain, and Kuwait. To the north and west is the Levant, which includes Jordan, Israel, Palestine (sometimes called the Palestinian Territories), Syria, and Egypt. North Africa, which runs across the top of the African continent along the Mediterranean, includes Libya, Tunisia, Algeria, and Morocco. Almost all regional states are members of the Arab League, with the exceptions of Syria, Iran, and Israel.

The Middle East has been an influential and important area throughout human history. Once home to some of mankind's earliest great civilizations, including Babylon and Mesopotamia, modern Middle Eastern countries include areas that saw large-scale growth and development as **Silk Road** trade stops. Today, it is home to some of the world's largest oil reserves, and it has been subject to a great deal of turmoil and unrest.

The region was first united under the Muslim Umayyad Empire, a **caliphate** that at its height spread from Spain to India. Other caliphates followed, including the Abbasid and the Mamluk, before the Ottomans of modern-day Turkey established their empire in the mid-1400s. The Ottomans controlled most of the modern Middle East, while the Persian Empire controlled the area now known as Iran and Arabia, including modern-day Saudi Arabia and other Gulf states, and allowed for varying degrees of independence over the centuries.

The Ottoman Empire collapsed after World War I, with official dissolution in 1922. At that time, the Empire was divided between the French and the British through the Sykes-Picot agreement, and the lines we think of as modern Middle Eastern boundaries were drawn. This agreement has been the source of much controversy over the years, with some considering it responsible for many of the rivalries that have led to instability because it did not recognize the naturally occurring boundaries between peoples and tribes. After this agreement, the French took control of Lebanon, Syria, and northern Iraq, while the British took control of Jordan, southern Iraq, and Palestine, where they would soon establish the state of Israel.

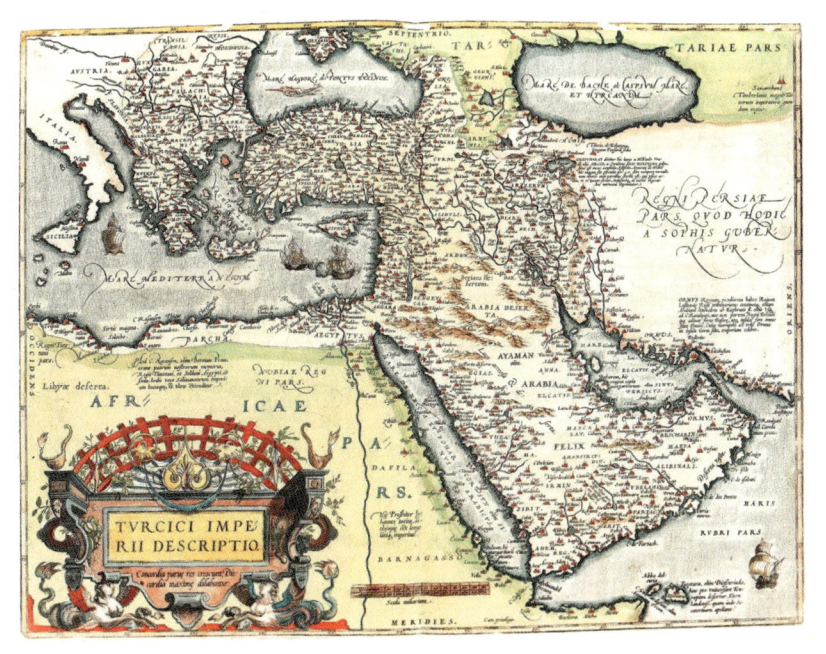

Much of the modern Middle East was part of the Ottoman Empire, shown here. The empire was governed from Constantinople, present-day Istanbul.

In North Africa, the French controlled Algeria, Morocco, and Tunisia from the mid-to-late 1800s, while the British occupied Egypt in the 1880s. In Iran, or Persia, the collapse of the Qajar Dynasty in the early 1900s was due in part to a British and Russian agreement to divide the country into spheres of influence, with the British controlling the south. After the fall of the Qajars and the withdrawal of Soviet forces, the Pahlavi Dynasty was established in 1925 under military strongman Reza Pahlavi, with support from the British.

It wasn't until the mid-to-late twentieth century that Middle Eastern states became independent, although many have since struggled to establish healthy democracies. That does not mean that the political system in every Middle Eastern country is the same, though. Monarchies, authoritarian regimes, **theocracies**, and democracies exist side-by-side, and within most governments there are varying degrees of representation and public engagement. The people of the Middle East have also fought long and hard to ensure their voices are heard and their governments are representative.

Although similar in some ways, the politics of each country in the Middle East and North Africa are very different. Some are monarchies, ruled over by a king or with the help of a parliament. Others are democracies, where presidents and representatives lead the country. Still others are somewhere between the two, with strong federal governments led by authoritarian figures. In countries like Jordan and Iran, the political system is made up of many voices, while in others, like Saudi Arabia and Egypt, one family or party holds all power. In Libya and Syria, attempts at reform have dissolved into crisis, while in Tunisia, political change was carried out while maintaining stability.

Politics in the Middle East are often overshadowed by considerable threats, including extremism and **non-state actors**, such as the Islamic State of Iraq and Syria (ISIS) or al-Qaeda. These groups, which operate outside the political system and threaten the legitimacy of central governments, undermine security with acts of terrorism and thrive in countries experiencing extreme unrest. Syria and Libya have become hotbeds for such activity, while neighboring states work to ensure the turmoil does not spread across their borders.

This book will explore the many differences and similarities that make the Middle East and North Africa a vibrant, fascinating, and complex place. The following chapters discuss the recent political history of each country, the challenges these governments face, and the ways they are working to resolve these issues. The final chapter highlights some important figures who have made the Middle East and North Africa what it is today, including politicians, religious leaders, and non-state actors.

The British occupied much of the Middle East during both World Wars. Here, soldiers arrive in Baghdad, Iraq.

1

The History of Geography, Government, and Conflict across the Middle East

The modern Middle East and North Africa took shape following World War I. During the 1920s, French and British officials drew boundaries and carved out areas of influence; prior to this time, the region had been governed as a whole by the Ottoman Empire. This chapter discusses the geographic and political history of each country in the twentieth century.

The Gulf

Bahrain

A neighbor of Qatar in the Persian Gulf, Bahrain is a small island country with a complicated history of foreign intervention and regional rivalry. The British controlled the island with varying degrees of authority throughout the nineteenth and early twentieth centuries, despite recognizing Bahraini independence in 1913. Like other regional states, Bahrain became a British protectorate, meaning the country was unable to form relations with foreign governments without British permission. Britain also controlled customs and trade, and held exclusive access to Bahrain's oil industry.

In 1935, Bahrain became home to Britain's primary military base in the region. The British maintained an active role in Bahrain's affairs until 1971, when a Treaty of Friendship officially ended Britain's formal role in the country. The former Administrative Council, a twelve-person committee run by a president, transitioned to the Council of State and soon after became the emir's cabinet.

A newly written constitution included a provision for two elected legislative bodies, called the Constituent Assembly and the National Assembly. But in 1975, the emir dissolved the National Assembly, and popular demonstrations in the early 1990s launched a decade of instability. The government experienced numerous shuffles during that time, and the decade culminated in a failed coup.

Iran

The twentieth century saw unprecedented changes in Iran. In the early 1900s, Britain and Russia divided the country into spheres of influence. The discovery of oil in Iran made the country strategically important for the British, particularly as reliance on oil grew during the first half of the century. But British exploitation of Iranian oil led to a great deal of resentment among average Iranians, many of whom worked for British companies in poor and unsafe conditions.

In 1952, Iranians voted for the first time, electing Mohammed Mossadegh as prime minister. Mossadegh was a **populist** figure, running on a platform that emphasized national control of the oil industry and reforms that would provide Iran with more autonomy from Britain. But these promises made the British concerned that Mossadegh would force them out of the country.

In 1953, the British called on the CIA to stage a coup, known as Operation Ajax. The operation was successful, forcing Mossadegh into house arrest through staged protests. Following Operation Ajax, Mohammed Reza Shah consolidated power and began cracking down on dissidents, opponents, and political groups. To this day, Operation Ajax is considered one of the most significant events in Iranian history, and this direct interference in domestic affairs continues to fuel mistrust between Iran and the United States.

Among those the shah cracked down on was Ayatollah Ruhollah Khomeini, who was exiled to Iraq and later Paris due to his outspoken opposition to the shah's rule. A Shiite **cleric**,

Murals like this one, showing Iran's first Supreme Leader Ayatollah Ruhollah Khomeini, are common in Iran.

Khomeini was able to build support while in exile by recording tapes that were smuggled into Iran and played at mosques around the country. By the late 1970s, a large coalition was built between clerics, leftist movements, republicans, and other groups who opposed the shah. In 1978, mass protests brought millions into the streets and the Shah fled to the United States, stating that he was going there for cancer treatment. In his absence, Ayatollah Khomeini returned and founded the Islamic Republic, a theocratic state based in **sharia** law with elements of both authoritarian rule and representative government.

Iraq

Located in the center of the Middle East, Iraq experienced a great deal of change and turmoil in the twentieth and early twenty-first centuries. During World War I, the British seized Baghdad from the Ottoman Empire. In 1920, Britain established the country of Iraq, and the League of Nations, a precursor to the United Nations, approved. But when establishing boundaries, the British failed to take into account **provincial** relations, religious differences, and group identity. Many have expressed the opinion that the way Iraq was delineated fed existing rivalries and tensions.

The same year Iraq was declared a country, mass protests marked the beginning of the Great Iraqi Revolution, challenging British rule. One year later, King Faysal was crowned as the country's first monarch, although the British Mandate remained in place until 1932, when Iraq became an independent state. But independence was short-lived; in 1939 World War II began, and British forces reoccupied Iraq until the war ended in 1945.

In 1958, the monarchy was overthrown in a military coup, and Iraq became a republic in name. But in reality, a series of coups and assassinations made the next twenty years unstable. In the late 1960s, the Baathist Party claimed and consolidated power, making Iraq a one-party state. In 1979, President Ahmed Hassan al-Bakr left office for health reasons, and his vice president, Saddam Hussein, took office. His almost thirty years in the presidency were marked by oppression and human rights violations. Under Hussein, Iraq spent most of the final decades of the twentieth century at war; the Iran-Iraq War lasted from 1980 to 1988, while Hussein's invasion of Kuwait launched the Gulf War in the 1990s. He remained in power until the United States led an invasion of Iraq in 2003.

Kuwait

Located between Saudi Arabia and Iraq, Kuwait became a British protectorate in 1899. The country remained under British control until 1961, and the first half of the twentieth century saw the development of Kuwait's oil industry and large-scale infrastructure growth.

Since independence, the country has struggled to find a balance between the ruling monarchy, headed by an emir, or Muslim leader, and representative government. Under a draft constitution, a parliament called the National Assembly was established in 1963, but the body has been dissolved multiple times by the emir in the name of national interest.

Tension between Kuwait and Iraq led to an international crisis in the early 1990s, when Saddam Hussein invaded the country, claiming it as part of Iraq. In 1991, the United States led a coalition against Iraq, marking the first Gulf War. With Iraqi forces pushed out of Kuwait, **martial law** was declared for three months, following which elections for a new National Assembly were called. But by 1999, the body was dissolved once again, with subsequent elections resulting in major wins for those opposed to the government.

Oman

Located along the southeastern edge of the Arabian Peninsula, Oman is home to one of the longest ruling governments in the region. The Al Bu Said dynasty gained control of the Omani empire in 1749 and has been in power ever since.

Oman became a British protectorate in the late nineteenth century but was able to maintain a large degree of autonomy. In 1913, the country was divided when opposition forces claimed the interior, splitting it from coastal areas under control of the capital, Muscat. An agreement was brokered by the British in 1920 that ended the conflict by recognizing the autonomy of the rebelling area. In 1954, clashes broke out between the government and those who held the interior and, by 1959, control of the country was once again in the hands of the Sultanate. A ten-year rebellion in the south, beginning in 1965 and continuing intermittently until 1975, also threatened central governance.

Like other countries in the region, oil was a driving force of development in the twentieth century. Oil reserves were found in Oman in 1964, with extraction beginning in 1967. Oil revenue made it possible for Sultan Qaboos, who took control in a bloodless coup in 1970, to pursue an agenda of economic and social development, investing in key infrastructure and industry while expanding voting rights and education. Under Sultan Qaboos, who rules today, Oman ended the 1990s in strong economic and international standing, with strong relationships with neighbors as well as military partnerships with the countries like the United Kingdom and the United States.

Qatar

Qatar is a small peninsula off the coast of Saudi Arabia. The emir of Qatar invited the Ottoman Empire to establish a presence in the area in the 1800s, and following the collapse of the Ottoman Empire, a similar agreement was put in place with the British. From 1916 to 1971, the British guaranteed the protection of Qatar in exchange for control over the country's foreign affairs.

In 1973, Khalifa bin Hamad al-Thani unseated the sitting ruler in a successful coup. He was later deposed by his own son, Hamad bin Khalifa al-Thani, in another coup. The throne passed to Hamad's son, Tamim bin Hamad al-Thani, in 2013, when his father abdicated.

In the late 1990s, Qatar began positioning itself as a media hub with the founding of Al Jazeera, an Arabic language news station funded by the government that has grown into a major international news company with multiple branches in other languages, including English.

Saudi Arabia

The largest country in the Arabian Peninsula, Saudi Arabia was established in 1932, following a thirty-year effort by the House of Saud, or the Al Saud family, to establish a kingdom. The monarchy founded in 1932 continues to rule the country today, with the throne passing from father to son.

In 1936, oil was found along the coast, and within three years, Saudi Arabia began exporting it. This led to a windfall for the royal family and made Saudi Arabia a key player in the growing oil industry. From 1939 to 1953, revenue from oil exports grew from $7 million per year to a staggering $200 million per year, becoming the key source of income for the country. Saudi Arabia helped found the Organization of Petroleum Exporting Countries in 1960, and the organization remains the primary body governing the oil trade.

Saudi Arabia was largely stable during the twentieth century, enjoying international alliances due to their importance in the oil trade and willingness to partner militarily with countries like the United States. But while the country has not experienced regime change, they have been accused of suppressing dissidents and opposition.

The Saudi royal family has long been aligned with Wahhabism, a conservative **sect** of Islam often associated with extremist groups like al-Qaeda. Wahhabism has influenced domestic policies since Saudi Arabia was founded, most visibly in the treatment of women.

Along with requiring substantial veiling when in public, women are not allowed to drive and only received the right to vote in 2015.

United Arab Emirates (UAE)

The United Arab Emirates, or the UAE, is a **federation** of seven monarchies sharing a border with Saudi Arabia and Oman. Abu Dhabi, Ras al-Khaymah, Ajman, Dubai, Fujayrah, Sharjah, and Umm al-Qaywayn were under British control until 1971. After independence, the kingdoms, all of which are small, decided to form the UAE. Each monarchy retains a great deal of independence, and all seven rulers sit on the Supreme Council of Rulers, which elects a president, prime minister, and cabinet.

Rich in oil and natural gas, the UAE is one of the wealthiest and most well developed states in the Middle East. It has become a hub for international business, and Dubai has become an iconic global city, home to structures like the Burj Khalifa, the tallest building in the world. But while the country has invested heavily in education, health care, and other key industries, authoritarian rule remains the norm. The country had their first elections in 2006, in which a very small group of people were allowed to vote for an advisory council.

Yemen

Along the southwestern edge of the Arabian Peninsula, Yemen was once two states, North and South Yemen. The two unified in 1990, but tensions remained between the government and separatist forces. In 1994, an uprising in the south led to a brief civil conflict, which temporarily solidified central rule.

Yemen has long been faced with instability, giving rise to extremist sects aligned with al-Qaeda and the so-called Islamic State. As a result of political instability, the state has struggled to develop. In 2014, it was declared a failed state following an uprising by Shia Houthi forces, which prompted the Sunni president to resign and flee. Since then, the state is mired in an ongoing civil war, and has regularly been targeted by drone strikes.

The Levant

Egypt

Egypt, in the northeastern corner of Africa, marks the boundary between the Middle East and North Africa. In 1882, the British occupied Egypt following a gradual takeover due to Egypt's economic hardship. The country built the Suez Canal in the 1860s, but the project left the government nearly bankrupt. The Suez Canal connects the Mediterranean to the Red Sea, and being able to manage that passage was an economic windfall for the British. Egypt became an official British protectorate in 1914.

Egypt formally gained independence in 1922, but Britain maintained significant influence until the 1950s. During World War II, Britain used Egypt as its primary military base of operations, but by the late 1940s, anti-British anger was growing. In 1952 anti-British riots marked a turning point in Egyptian politics, and a military coup that same year led to the establishment of a republic. In 1956, Gamal Abdel Nasser succeeded the country's first president, Muhammad Najib, and soon after nationalized the Suez Canal. An attempt by the British to invade and secure the

President Gamal Abdel Nasser was a populist leader in Egypt. In office, he challenged Western control of his country.

Suez Canal failed, and Nasser became an international symbol of opposition to western powers. At home, Nasser combined efforts to kick-start the economy with strict repression of political opposition.

In 1970, Nasser was succeeded by Anwar Sadat, who held office for eleven years. Although he established a multiparty political system, Sadat did little to strengthen the country. He signed a peace treaty with Israel, a decision that secured an alliance with the United States and guaranteed aide money for Egypt, but enraged anti-Israel political opponents. In 1981, Sadat was assassinated, and his vice president, Hosni Mubarak, became president. Mubarak, who controlled Egypt until an **Arab Spring** revolution unseated him in 2011, oversaw harsh censorship and tight control of the political process, staging elections in which he won without opposition.

Israel

In 1917, the British came into control of Palestine, a small area along the Mediterranean. That year, Britain also released the Balfour Declaration, a statement expressing their support for the establishment of a Jewish state in the area. Jewish migration from Europe began soon after, with numbers increasing significantly following the Holocaust. Israel declared itself an independent state in 1948 and was recognized by the international community almost immediately. Since then, the country has been closely aligned with the west, particularly the United States.

But Israel has not been without controversy. Shortly after migration began, it became clear that establishing a state where people, the Palestinians, were already living would be difficult.

Conflict began almost immediately, with refugees pouring into nearby states. The same year Israel declared independence, the first Arab-Israeli War resulted in Israel claiming more land than was originally agreed to in the British **partition** plan. In 1967, the Six-Day War would have much the same impact, with Israel claiming territory that had been held by Lebanon, Egypt, and Jordan.

The Israel-Palestine conflict is one of the longest running crises in the region, with regular fighting occurring between Israeli forces and Palestinians in Lebanon, the West Bank, and the Gaza Strip. Reaching an agreement that will bring peace has been a priority for the international community for decades, but a solution has yet to be found.

Jordan

Jordan, a country with a strong tribal and **nomadic** tradition, shares a border with Saudi Arabia, Iraq, Lebanon, and Israel. First established as Transjordan and held under British control after World War I, the state of Jordan was recognized as independent in 1946. Two years later, the state of Israel was officially recognized between Jordan and the Mediterranean, and thousands of Palestinians fled to Jordanian territory. During the Six-Day War of 1967, between Israel and multiple Arab powers, Jordan saw another large influx of refugees, adding strain to an already sluggish economic situation. Tension between the government and refugee populations, who mostly live in camps, has been an issue for Jordan since it was recognized.

Jordan's Film Industry

Fans of films like Indiana Jones may recognize the landscape in Jordan—parts of the film *Indiana Jones and the Last Crusade* were filmed at the historic Petra Monastery in the Jordanian desert. With few resources and little economic output, Jordan has worked to establish the country as a go-to for Hollywood shoots. King Abdullah II is a film fan, and as such has invested in making Jordan appealing for the film industry. Movies like *The Hurt Locker*, *The Devil's Double*, and *The Martian* were filmed there. In addition to providing the perfect desert landscapes for movies, Hollywood brings much needed income to the country. These shoots also employ a great deal of local talent, including extras and crew. According to the Royal Film Commission, film crews are made up of about 98 percent Jordanians on shoots in the country, and each day of shooting brings in about 100,000 Jordanian dollars. Other countries, including India, the United Kingdom, and Brazil, have also used Jordanian locations in film shoots. Despite unrest in the region, Jordan remains a popular destination for filmmakers.

A constitutional monarchy, Jordan is ruled by a king and parliament. The government has aligned itself closely with the west and signed a peace treaty with Israel in 1994. Jordan does not have many natural resources and relies heavily on international aid to prop up the economy. As a result, development has been slow, and instability in the region has made it difficult to increase growth. Meanwhile, discontent with the lack of reform observed throughout the twentieth century and economic hardship led to semiregular riots, protests, and other demonstrations.

Lebanon

Lebanon, formed after World War I by bringing several provinces together under one jurisdiction, was controlled by the French until 1945. Shortly thereafter, signs of instability became clear as opposition to the government resulted in a brief civil war in 1958. Like Jordan, Lebanon's stability was challenged by the influx of Palestinian refugees following the creation of the state of Israel. In 1975, an opposition group attacked a bus, killing twenty-seven Palestinians and launching a civil war that lasted until 1990. During the civil war, Syria and Israel became involved, and Israel invaded southern Lebanon in 1982.

Although the civil war ended in 1990, southern Lebanon has become a stronghold for Islamist pro-Palestinian group Hezbollah, considered a terrorist organization by the West. As a result of their presence and activities in Israeli territory, Israel and Lebanon have been engaged in conflict regularly since the 1990s.

Palestine

Palestine, or the Palestinian Territories, includes the West Bank to the east of Israel and the Gaza Strip, bordering Israel, the Mediterranean, and Egypt's Sinai Peninsula. The Palestinian Authority governs the West Bank, although most control of the area is held by Israel, which has occupied the area since 1967. The Gaza Strip is controlled by Hamas, a political and militant group considered a terrorist organization by the West that has ruled the small area since being elected in 2006. That same year, Israel agreed to end its occupation of the Gaza Strip, but has since held the area under embargo, giving rise to a network of black-market tunnels into Egypt through which Palestinians bring in needed food, construction materials, medical supplies, and fuel.

Palestine is not formally recognized as a **sovereign** state, although the Palestinian Authority has taken the question to the United Nations' General Assembly and been recognized by many international governments. But the continued Israel-Palestine conflict has meant that Palestine has little control over its own land, and militant extremists have engaged Israeli forces in numerous conflicts and carried out terrorist attacks around the world throughout the twentieth and early twenty-first centuries. Although some areas of the West Bank have been able to develop, Israeli checkpoints, restricted roads, and settlements, as well as the continued restriction of goods and services into the heavily bombed Gaza, have made it difficult for the territories to establish themselves as a state.

Syria

In the northern Middle East and sharing a border with Turkey, Syria gained its independence from the Ottoman Empire by force in 1917, with the assistance of British forces. Emir Faisal, who would be crowned King of Syria in 1920, supported self-rule, and called for elections for the Syrian National Congress. But later that year, Syria was granted to France under the same mandate that granted them control of Lebanon, and French forces in Damascus forced King Faisal to flee.

In 1925, nationalism swept Syria, and the French struggled to hold onto control. A draft constitution was rejected by the French in 1928, and protests against their rule began. In 1936, France agreed to grant Syria independence, but during World War II, British and French troops occupied the country. It wasn't until 1946 that French forces fully left Syria.

Following French withdrawal, Syria struggled to maintain a dynamic political system. Coups unseated several governments, political parties sought to claim sole power, and multiple conflicts with Israel occurred. In 1973, Hafez al-Assad was elected president, a post he held until his death in 2000, when his son, Bashar al-Assad, succeeded him. Throughout the final quarter of the twentieth century, riots and protests took place, and the state cracked down on opposition groups like the Muslim Brotherhood as the Assad family consolidated power.

North Africa

Algeria

Under the Ottoman Empire, Algeria, like other modern countries in the Middle East and North Africa, was a semiautonomous province. But in 1830, France captured the capital, Algiers, claiming it as a colony. Algeria won its independence in a war that lasted from 1954 to 1962 and resulted in the death of more than one million Algerians.

Following independence, rival factions within the country, which is 80 percent Saharan Desert, began fighting over control. After a series of coups, a civil war broke out in 1991, pitting the government against Islamist rebels. The Islamist FIS (Islamic Salvation Front) party was projected to do well in elections that year, and in response the military stepped in to suppress them, launching the almost ten-year conflict. The civil war lasted until 1999, when then-new president Abdelaziz Bouteflika began a process of national reconciliation.

Libya

Unlike other regional states, Libya was held by Italy from 1911, when the Italians seized control from the Ottoman Empire. For the next twenty years, a growing group of rebels from various tribal groups fought against Italian rule, but ultimately Italian forces crushed that insurgency in 1931. During World War II,

Protesters clash with police during the Algerian Civil War, which lasted from 1954 to 1962.

Italy lost Libya to the Allies and, after the war, the country was divided between the British and the French. Libya was declared independent in 1951, following which it was ruled by King Idris.

In 1969, Colonel Muammar Qaddafi unseated King Idris in a coup and set about aligning Libya with Arab states. He also promoted **nationalization**, claiming control of the oil industry. By 1979, the chaos and arbitrary, repressive governing that Qaddafi would become known for was becoming clear. In the 1980s, he clashed with international powers, including the United States, which carried out bombings of Tripoli and other cities in 1986 after Libya was allegedly involved in an attack on a discotheque in Berlin, Germany. In 1988, Libya was suspected of being involved in the bombing of an airplane over the town of Lockerbie, Scotland. The 1990s were marked by more international provocation and internal chaos.

Morocco

In 1912, Morocco became a French protectorate, with Spain policing a small coastal area of influence. Starting in the early 1920s, uprisings against French and Spanish rule were increasingly common until, in 1943, an official party of independence was established. Nationalism and unrest over foreign rule forced the French to grant Morocco independence in 1956, although the Spanish remained in their coastal protectorate until 1975 when Moroccan volunteer forces entered the area.

After European forces left Morocco, the country became engaged in a conflict with Algeria and Mauritania over ownership of the former Spanish protectorates, called Western Sahara.

Although all three states agreed to a ceasefire in the early 1990s, the status of Western Sahara is still disputed.

Following independence, King Hassan took power after the death of his father, but he struggled with establishing a more democratic state. Elections were called and canceled multiple times in the second half of the twentieth century. In 1962, a new constitution created a bicameral, or two-house, parliament. But the king declared a state of emergency in 1965 due to unrest, and the parliament was dissolved. It was recalled shortly thereafter but, in 1972, a new constitution approved by referendum did away with one of the houses of parliament and outlined more clearly the balance of powers between the branches of government. In both 1992 and 1996, constitutional amendments restored the second house of parliament and expanded the legislature's power.

In 1999, Hassan passed away, and his son, Mohammed VI, took the throne. Although he promised reforms, Morocco was among the states that saw widespread protests in the 2011 Arab Spring uprisings.

Tunisia

Tunisia became a French protectorate in the late 1880s and held power until after World War II. In 1934, Habib Bourguiba founded the first independence party, called Neo-Destour. Although calls for independence were common over the next two decades, the French did not grant Tunisia independence until 1956.

The French had originally worked out an agreement under which Tunisia would be ruled as a constitutional monarchy, with the royal **bey** working with elected representatives. But Bourguiba and Lamine Bey agreed to structure elections in a way that guaranteed Bourguiba's party would come to power and he would become prime minister. In 1957, the monarchy was abolished, and Tunisia became a republic.

Bouguiba ruled Tunisia for the next thirty-one years, instituting vast changes to the political culture and economy. Under his guidance, Tunisia became a secular and populist state, but not one with democratic representation. Bourguiba was declared President for Life in 1975. Tunisia was a one-party state, with a few sanctioned parties allowed to run in elections in 1981 although the Neo-Destour Party won all seats. When Bourguiba was declared unable to rule due to medical concerns in 1987, General Zine al-Abidine Ben Ali became president and would hold the post until 2011, when popular protests in Tunisia started the Arab Spring.

Although Ben Ali initially made some reforms and limited presidential powers, unrest in 1989 prompted him to crack down on demonstrations and reinstate his Bourguiba-era authoritarianism. He was subsequently elected to multiple terms, and his regime was marked by various human rights violations. High unemployment, repression, and corruption drove unrest that would eventually unseat him.

The House of Saud has ruled Saudi Arabia since 1932. King Salman inherited the throne from his brother in 2015.

2

Modern-Day Geography, Government, and Conflict in the Gulf

The Gulf, which includes Iran, Iraq, Kuwait, Saudi Arabia, United Arab Emirates, Qatar, Bahrain, Yemen, and Oman, borders the Red Sea in the west and the Arabian Sea in the east. The area is home to some of the world's largest oil reserves, making it extremely wealthy. Like the rest of the Middle East and North Africa, the Gulf is primarily Sunni Muslim, except for Iran and Bahrain, which are Shiite-majority countries. While most states in the Gulf have monarchs who still oversee the government, democratic movements have been active in the area, including Iran's Green Movement of 2009 and Bahrain's Arab Spring protests of 2011. The most pivotal events and concerns in the area in the twenty-first century have been public protests, the Iranian nuclear crisis, and rivalry between regional states.

Iran

The Iranian government is built on religious ideology put forward by Ayatollah Ruhollah Khomeini, the leader of the 1979 Islamic Revolution and the country's first Supreme Leader. Khomeini's philosophy, set out in the book *The Rule of the Jurisprudence*, called for the guardianship of the state to be held by a high-ranking cleric and for the laws of the state to be guided by sharia, or Islamic law. His philosophy was codified in the 1979 constitution that established the Islamic Republic of Iran.

The Supreme Leader sits at the top of a complex political hierarchy, with a combination of elected and appointed positions. The appointed Expediency Council is the advisory body for the Supreme Leader and mediates disagreements between the parliament and the Guardian Council. The president and parliament are elected by popular vote. The Guardian Council, a twelve-member body made up of six jurists and six clerics, is appointed by the judiciary and approved by the parliament. It is responsible for ensuring that laws reflect both Islamic values and the constitution. The Assembly of Experts is an elected group of clerics responsible for appointing the Supreme Leader and overseeing his work, with the power to remove him from office if needed.

Iran's regional and global relations are defined largely by a key contradiction; although Iran sees itself as heir to a legacy of greatness, including a history that spans Alexander the Great, Cyrus the Great, and the Persian Empire, the country has experienced extreme hardship and isolation since 1979. As a result, Iran has tried to secure influence in states like Syria and Iraq, and among Gulf Shiite populations. The government, which was established during the 1979 revolution, is divided between hardline, conservative elements and moderate voices, leading to tension among some of the highest offices in the regime. Human rights activists have condemned the country for its use of torture against dissidents, gender inequality, minority persecution, support for groups like Hamas, and censorship, among other concerns.

The twenty-first century began with a more moderate government in the Iranian capital of Tehran, run by both the Supreme Leader Ali Khamenei and President Mohammad Khatami. Khatami, a reform-minded cleric, was able to usher in some changes to the conservative government, and Iran's economy was strong. But in 2005, Tehran mayor and political outsider Mahmoud Ahmadinejad was elected president, and existing tensions between Iran and the international community, which Khatami was largely able to smooth over diplomatically, were strained by the new president's outlandish and hostile rhetoric.

Domestically, the Ahmadinejad years saw Iran largely isolated due to both the government's unwillingness to negotiate an end to the debate surrounding its nuclear program and his frequent aggressive public statements. Iran's economy struggled under

Iranian president Hassan Rouhani

international **sanctions**, which were imposed by the United States and European countries due to the nuclear program.

In 2009, Ahmadinejad was up for election against Reformist candidate Mir Hossein Mousavi, a former prime minister who ran on a campaign of change. Polls showed the election was close, but when the results came in shortly after polls closed, Ahmadinejad was declared the winner. Mousavi and fellow candidate Mehdi Karroubi called their supporters to the street to demand a recount and protest the outcome, but the government responded with violence. Street demonstrations continued for months, but the crackdown carried out by government forces and state-supported mobs soon brought them to an end, particularly following the house arrest of Mousavi and Karroubi.

During Ahmadinejad's second term, the country continued to experience the impact of sanctions, including the complete collapse of their currency, the rial, and shortages of medical supplies and other goods. But in 2012, the election of moderate cleric Hassan Rouhani ushered in significant changes in Iran's approach to global affairs, and in 2015 his government was able to negotiate an agreement with the United States and allies that brought the decade-long nuclear crisis to an end. This allowed for the lifting of sanctions and the recovery of the Iranian economy.

Iraq

The constitution of Iraq defines the country as a representative, democratic, federal parliamentary republic, meaning that the federal government holds central control and is governed by representatives chosen through elections. The constitution also names Islam as the official state religion, and the law is shaped by a combination of Islamic law and civil law. Unlike Iran, clerics do not have a prominent or guaranteed role in the federal government, although prominent religious leaders do have regional influence among their followers.

The Iraqi government is overseen by a prime minister and a president, both of whom are elected by the parliament (called the Council of Representatives of Iraq). The prime minister holds most executive power and selects a council of ministers that functions much like the United States's presidential cabinet. The president is responsible for overseeing the legislative branch and ensuring laws follow the constitution. The public votes for the Council of Representatives.

For Iraq, one of the lingering problems the country has faced since independence has been overcoming divisions between religious and ethnic communities. Shias have long made up the religious majority of Iraq, although Sunnis held power before the US-led invasion of Iraq in 2003. Saddam Hussein and the Baathist party were anti-Kurdish and largely anti-Shia, and their thirty-five years in power were a time of oppression. Populations that long felt they were marginalized sought power after Hussein fell, which led to conflict with the Sunnis who had been in power. That conflict has exacerbated instability and assisted in the rise of extremist group the Islamic State of Iraq and Syria (ISIS), also called Daesh, Islamic State in Iraq and the Levant (ISIL), or Islamic State.

In 2003, Iraq was invaded by the United States under suspicion that the country had weapons of mass destruction, including biological and chemical weapons, an allegation that was later found to be false. After a controversial campaign to win over the public, the Bush administration launched a campaign against Saddam Hussein's government, ending his rule and occupying the country.

Called the Assassins' Gate, this archway is one of four points of entry into the Green Zone in Baghdad, Iraq.

US forces withdrew from Iraq in 2011, with advisors and some personnel remaining to assist with recovery and transition.

In 2005, a new constitution was drafted to establish a new, democratic state. It established the federal system described earlier in this section. In it, Iraqi **Kurds** received an autonomous region, known as Iraqi Kurdistan. This official recognition followed many years of armed conflict, including the Iraqi government's use of chemical weapons against Kurds in 1988. Kurdish leadership has since expressed interest in full independence.

In 2006, Nouri al-Maliki was selected to be the first Prime Minister of the new Iraqi government, marking the first time that a Shia Muslim had ruled Iraq since the 1100s. His selection for the post was a significant moment for Iraqi Shiites, a minority population long marginalized and closely aligned with neighboring Iran. But by the 2010s, concern was mounting that al-Maliki's government was ignoring the needs of Sunni Muslims, thus provoking a simmering sense of disenfranchisement that would help give rise to the rise of ISIS. In 2014, al-Maliki stepped down and Haider al-Abadi filled the office. Al-Maliki has since served as vice president.

Saudi Arabia

Saudi Arabia is an absolute monarchy, meaning that the king holds all power. In January 2015, King Abdullah passed away, and the crown passed to his brother, Salman, signaling the continuation of the hereditary monarchy. Salman is the final son of Abdulaziz, the first king of Saudi Arabia, and his heir apparent will become the first of the next generation to take the throne.

The king appoints a crown prince, who assists with his duties and is the presumed heir to the throne. The king also appoints a 22-member council of ministers and a 150-member consultative council. Both groups advise the king on legislative and state matters, but the king makes all final decisions. The king also serves as the highest court of the land and can overrule lower court decisions. The public is able to vote for local councils, which have limited authority in local matters.

The 2010s have been markedly difficult for the once stable country. Low oil prices threaten the country's largest source of income, and ongoing conflict in neighboring states have strained Saudi security. Saudi forces are also engaged in neighboring Yemen's civil war, and their tense status quo with Iran has been strained consistently. Controversy has also plagued the religious pilgrimage of *hajj*, a large source of revenue for Saudi Arabia and one of the most important pillars of Islam.

During the Arab Spring uprisings in early 2011, the Saudi government was proactive and promised additional benefits for citizens worth about $127 billion. It was an attempt to head off unrest, but when demonstrations began in March of that year, the government stood by the formal ban on protests and cracked down on dissidents. Although activists have organized small demonstrations in the years since, security forces have continued to crack down on activity.

The state is closely aligned with Wahhabism, the extremely conservative sect of Islam that is associated with the ideology of al-Qaeda. Although Saudi Arabia does not have a constitution, a royal decree called the Basic Law of Saudi Arabia refers to the Quran as the basis for all governance. The law is based in Islamic sharia law.

Saudi Arabia has seen significant challenges to their human rights record in the twenty-first century, and the country's strict, conservative treatment of women has drawn harsh criticism from countries around the world. In 2015, women received the right to vote for the first time but are still not allowed to drive and are restricted from traveling without the permission of male relatives. In addition, the use of public executions, crackdowns on protesters, the monarch's tight control on power, and censorship draw frequent condemnation.

Gulf Monarchies

Bahrain, Kuwait, Qatar, UAE, and Oman are all monarchies to various degrees. These small states are ruled by monarchs, but some have elements of democracy at some level of the federal government.

In Bahrain, the public votes for one house of parliament, called the Chamber of Deputies, while the king appoints the other house, called the Shura Council. Both houses need to approve a bill before the king ratifies it. If the king decides not to approve a bill, it returns to the parliament, where it must be approved by two-thirds of both houses.

Kuwait has a system of checks and balances that allows the public to have a considerable voice in politics. The fifty-member parliament, called the National Assembly, is chosen by popular vote. The parliament is able to overrule royal vetoes, and the independent Constitutional Court can overrule royal decree to dissolve the parliament. Kuwait's court system is often called the most independent in the Gulf.

Qatar passed a constitution in 2003 that expanded the parliamentary Consultative Council from thirty-five royally appointed members to forty-five elected members, but elections have been postponed repeatedly, and the legislature has yet to change. Elections are expected to be held in 2019.

Dubai

Dubai is the largest city in the United Arab Emirates and one of the most expensive cities in the world. Located along the Gulf Coast, the city is home to some of the most ambitious architecture undertaken in recent years, including the Burj Khalifa, the tallest skyscraper in the world. Since the 1960s, the city has emerged as a global center of trade, tourism, and industry. The city has established trade-friendly practices, including free zones that have very low tax rates. This has allowed centers of industry, including the Dubai Internet City and the Dubai Media City, to become thriving business zones. Today, major media companies like the BBC and CNN have bureaus in Dubai, and international companies like Hewlett Packard and Microsoft have offices there. But Dubai is far from an equally prosperous city. While the city has become extremely wealthy, it has also been accused of various human rights violations. International human rights groups have found that foreign workers are often made to work in unsafe conditions for low pay. In 2015, Human Rights Watch found that Dubai police have allegedly tortured detainees, and that domestic workers have few protections against abuse by their employers.

In Oman, the public elects an advisory council, providing guidance to the sultan. Sultan Qaboos bin Said of Oman is the longest-serving leader in the Middle East, and no laws can be issued in the country without his decree. The country's legal code sets out defined civil liberties and freedoms although, without any form of checks and balances, the leadership of Oman regularly ignores them.

The kingdoms that make up the UAE, like Saudi Arabia, are also absolute monarchies. The emir of Abu Dhabi is designated as the president of the UAE, and the emir of Dubai is the prime minister; these positions are passed down through hereditary lines. In 2006, the UAE convened the Federal National Council. Half of the forty-member council is elected, while the UAE's emirs appoint the other half. However, this council fulfills a largely advisory role and does not make laws itself.

The Arab Spring

In 2011, popular uprisings swept North Africa and the Middle East, drastically reshaping the region. The Gulf was not untouched by protest, with public discontent over economic inequality and political repression boiling over into calls for reforms and democratic governance.

In February 2011, Bahrain, a Shiite majority country ruled by a Sunni monarchy, saw large numbers take to the streets and set up a camp in the capital city, Manama, to demand greater political freedom and the end to the hereditary monarchy. But these protests were short-lived. Within six weeks, the Bahraini government requested assistance from the Gulf Cooperation

Protests in Bahrain were violently ended in 2011, with help from Saudi Arabian forces.

Council, a body that facilitates relations between states on the Arab Peninsula. Saudi Arabia sent one thousand troops and the UAE sent five hundred to help crack down on protesters, with thousands arrested and around thirty people killed. The crackdown drew harsh criticism from Iran, a state that has been accused of seeking influence with Bahrain's Shia population, and the international community. Although protests have continued sporadically ever since, the government has shown a willingness to continue cracking down on dissident voices and a refusal to implement requested reforms.

Similar protests took place in Oman, with similar results. Demonstrations in cities across Oman were tolerated when they started in February 2011. But security forces moved in when a protest in the city of Sohar took a violent turn. In May, demonstrations were broken up in the capital of Muscat and other major cities, and Sultan Qaboos announced that the government would begin implementing reforms. One year later, however, the government responded to criticism by launching a wave of arrests, targeting bloggers and activists. Although all people arrested have since been released, Oman has struggled to address the inequality that led to the protests.

Yemen

Oman's neighbor, Yemen, was plunged into a civil war following protests in January 2011. Demonstrations against the thirty-three-year rule of President Ali Abd Allah Saleh continued even after he promised not to run for another term, and in response, the government launched a crackdown that killed an unknown number of people. Although Yemen brokered a deal with the Gulf Cooperation Council to end Saleh's presidency in April of that year, this action empowered opposition rebel groups, and clashes broke out in the capital of Sanaa. Saleh fled, and elections brought Abd Rabbuh Mansur Hadi to power in 2012.

Clashes escalated into a full civil war in early 2015, when Shiite Houthi rebels took control of Sanaa and declared themselves the official government. Both Hadi's supporters and the Houthis claim authority. The Sunni extremist group al-Qaeda in the Arab Peninsula has been active in the country, claiming a large stretch of land in the middle of the country. ISIS has also staked a claim in Yemen. Due to the presence of al-Qaeda forces, the United States has carried out drone strikes in Yemen, a controversial policy that has been blamed for a high number of civilian deaths. In early 2015, Yemen was declared a failed state, meaning it was unable to successfully govern itself. As of May 2016, it has been estimated that over six thousand people have been killed in the fighting.

Regional Relations

The states of the Arabian Peninsula have strong relationships, governed by the Gulf Cooperation Council (GCC), which was founded in 1981. Much like other regional unions, including the European Union, the GCC was developed to facilitate trade and private sector cooperation, as well as to create a military agreement to protect all member states. Yemen, Iraq, and Iran are not members of the GCC.

Relations in the Gulf are defined largely by the tension and rivalry between Iran and Saudi Arabia. These two countries represent different ends of the political, religious, and nationalist spectrum in the Middle East. Iran is ethnically Persian (with a Kurdish minority in the north), religiously Shia Muslim, and governed by a theocratic republican system that blends appointed

The hajj is an important religious pilgrimage made by Muslims, but it is also a source of controversy and tension.

and elected positions. Saudi Arabia is ethnically Arab, religiously Sunni, and ruled by an absolute monarchy. Their languages are also different, with Iranians speaking Farsi while Saudi Arabians speaks Arabic. Both states seek influence in the region more broadly, with Iran aligned closely with Iraq since 2003 while Saudi Arabia holds sway in the Gulf States, and their substantial oil reserves have led to economic competition.

As a result of these differences and their similar ambitions in the region, Iran and Saudi Arabia have had tense relations that have verged on hostilities. Disagreements range from accusations of interference in domestic affairs to a continued debate over the name of the Gulf itself, with Iran calling it the Persian Gulf while Saudi Arabia calls it the Arabian Gulf. Tensions reached a critical point in 2016, when diplomatic outreach that had been undertaken in recent years came to a halt. The breakdown was prompted by the large numbers of Iranians killed in 2015's hajj pilgrimage and the execution of Shiite cleric Sheikh Nimr al-Nimr by Saudi Arabia, as well as accusations that Iran had been spying on Saudi Arabia.

A key point of conflict between Saudi Arabia and Iran has been the hajj, an annual pilgrimage to Mecca that is one of the key tenets of Islam. The event draws millions from around the world to Saudi Arabia each year, including large numbers from Iran. But the large event is often overshadowed by tragedy, with many dying each year in stampedes and the collapse of infrastructure. In 2015, a stampede killed over two thousand pilgrims, including over four hundred Iranians. In response, Iran announced in 2016 that they would not be sending pilgrims to Mecca that year.

Poor relations between Iran and Saudi Arabia have impacted other regional countries, as well. In Bahrain, Yemen, Iraq, and Lebanon among other countries, a proxy conflict has pitted Iranian-backed militias against Saudi allies. Along with fostering instability in these states, the ongoing conflict between Iran and Saudi Arabia threatens Syrian peace talks and efforts to counter extremism.

Petra is a famous Jordanian heritage site. It has been used in numerous movies and is a UNESCO-protected site.

3

Modern-Day Geography, Government, and Conflict in the Levant

The Levant, which includes Jordan, Lebanon, Syria, Israel, Palestine, and Egypt, is located to the south of Turkey. It borders the Mediterranean Sea on the west and the Arabian Desert on the south, while Egypt makes up the northeastern tip of the African continent. The Levant is very religiously diverse, with Jews, Christians, Muslims, and sects of each living together. The area has struggled with long-term conflicts, including the Israel-Palestine conflict, and the Syrian civil war, and many refugees live in the region. But the area is also home to cosmopolitan cities, like Tel Aviv and Beirut, and the many cultural differences in the Levant have made it a vibrant part of the world.

Egypt

Egypt serves as a passage between the Middle East and North Africa. Located in the northeastern tip of Africa, the Sinai Peninsula is considered part of the Middle East. As a result, Egypt straddles Africa and Asia. Egypt borders Israel, Sudan, and Libya, and the Sinai Peninsula rests across from Jordan and Saudi Arabia in the Gulf of Aqaba. To the north, the Mediterranean Sea separates it from Turkey.

Like Tunisia, Libya, and Syria, Egypt experienced large-scale protests that upended a decades-long dictatorship in 2011. Hosni Mubarak came to power in 1981 and maintained control through staged elections until forced from office in January 2011. Under Mubarak, the political system had rewarded those who were loyal to him, both by providing power and by making his allies wealthy. During his time in office, Mubarak repressed dissent, controlled the press, marginalized opposition parties, and used a secret police force to carry out arrests and interrogations of activists or other opponents.

Popular protests broke out in early 2011, demanding the resignation of Mubarak, greater freedom, and economic opportunity. Like other countries in the Middle East and North Africa, Egypt's population is very young and well educated, and the lack of upward mobility created a growing sense of disenfranchisement among a

Arab Spring protests in Egypt unseated longtime ruler Hosni Mubarak in 2011.

huge part of the population. The military, rather than siding with Mubarak, chose to support the protestors. The military has long been popular and well respected among the public, and their support for demonstrations ensured that protests remained primarily peaceful, despite some pro-Mubarak groups agitating and using violence to discredit those calling for his resignation.

Hosni Mubarak stepped down in early February 2011, and the following month a referendum passed term limits, judicial supervision of elections, and other restrictions designed to ensure the next president followed democratic principles. A new parliament, called the People's Assembly, was elected the following year, and in May, Mohammed Morsi was elected president. Morsi, a member of the long marginalized Islamist party the Muslim Brotherhood, was not in office long; in June 2013, he was ousted by a military coup and the constitution was suspended. The following year, military officer Abdel Fattah al-Sisi was elected president.

Although the People's Assembly and president are elected by popular vote, concerns have been raised that the current system is similar to the system under Mubarak, in that the president has too much power with few checks and balances. Today, the military dominates the government through the presidency, and opposition figures and groups are largely marginalized once again.

Israel and Palestine

Israel and Palestine, discussed together due to their interconnected governance, comprise a small strip of land about the same size as Maryland. The area is bordered by the Mediterranean Sea on the west and Lebanon, Syria, Jordan, and Egypt on land. Israel makes up the bulk of the area, with the Gaza Strip in the southwest corner along the Mediterranean and the Sinai Peninsula, and the West Bank in the east bordering Jordan.

Israel, the Gaza Strip, and the West Bank are all governed by separate governments. Israel is a multiparty parliamentary system, with a president and a prime minister. The parliament, called the Knesset, is voted into office for four-year terms by popular elections. The Knesset selects the president, and the president nominates a prime minister who is suggested and approved by

Israeli Prime Minister Benjamin Netanyahu and PA leader Mahmoud Abbas are seen here meeting ahead of ongoing peace talks.

the Knesset. While the president serves as a ceremonial figure in Israeli politics, the prime minister is the functional head of the government, representing the country overseas and largely setting the tone for the country's politics.

The West Bank is governed by the Palestinian National Authority, which was set up in 1994 through the Oslo peace process. Although intended to only function for five years as an interim government, it continues to oversee affairs in the West Bank and is associated with the Palestinian Liberation Organization, an internationally recognized representative of the Palestinian people. The parliament, called the Palestinian Legislative Council, and the president are elected, and the prime minister is then nominated by the president.

The Gaza Strip is separated from the West Bank by Israeli territory. In 2006, Hamas won elections in the Gaza Strip, a controversial result due to Hamas's anti-Israel stance and their being considered a terrorist organization by many countries. The group is one of several pro-Palestinian organizations that has carried out attacks against Israel, and much of the international community does not recognize Hamas as legitimate leadership. Although the Palestinian National Authority was given jurisdiction over the area in 2014, Hamas continues to effectively rule. In response to the election of Hamas, Israel began an economic boycott that has left the Gaza Strip largely cut off from resources and trade.

The official status of the Palestinian territories is debated, with Palestinian leadership arguing that they should receive official statehood while Israel maintains a military occupation of the West Bank. In 2012, the United Nations unofficially recognized Palestine as a "non-member observer state," and 70 percent of UN member states have individually recognized its sovereignty. The legality of Israeli settlements, or small communities, in the West Bank has been heavily disputed, with some arguing that these pockets of Israeli presence undermine Palestinian sovereignty. The West Bank's political situation is further complicated by Israeli checkpoints, restricted access roads, and policies that allow the Israeli military to seize Palestinian lands and homes.

Palestinian activism has long been overshadowed by violence. Groups like Hamas, Fatah, and Lebanon's Hezbollah are just a few of the Levant-located organizations that have carried out attacks against Israel in the name of Palestinian liberation. Israel, in turn, has launched devastating attacks against Palestine, most recently in a large-scale military action in Gaza in 2014. Meanwhile, the Palestinian cause has become a rallying cry for Muslims who want to position themselves against the West and the United States, which is seen as Israel's greatest ally. Despite their many differences, the Iranian government and Islamist groups, including al-Qaeda and the Muslim Brotherhood, have all been vocal in their opposition to Israel. For some, this hostile environment justifies the continued Israeli military occupation on the grounds that the state of Israel is under threat from non-state actors and countries like Iran. Others make the case that Israeli policy only serves to fuel the sense of disenfranchisement and oppression that feeds support for groups like Hamas. Although internationally mediated peace negotiations have been ongoing for decades, an arrangement that ends the conflict has never been found.

Jordan

In the south of the Levant, Jordan shares a border with Saudi Arabia in the south and Iraq, Syria, and Israel in the east. Egypt and Jordan also face each other with a brief boundary along the Red Sea's Gulf of Aqaba. The country is primarily desert, which, along with the large refugee population in the country, has posed significant issues for the Jordanian economy.

Jordan, or the Hashemite Kingdom of Jordan, is a constitutional monarchy, with a king and a parliament called the National Assembly. The National Assembly has one house of elected members and another with members appointed by the king. Jordan also has a prime minister, who is appointed by the king, and an

King Abdullah II has ruled Jordan since 1999, when he inherited the throne from his father.

elected council of ministers to oversee state matters. The country is multiparty, with each parliament made up of various political and religious factions. But power ultimately lies with the king.

Politics in Jordan are influenced heavily by both the power of the king and the relationship between the state and tribes. Tribalism, or governance through tribes, was the political system that governed day-to-day affairs in the Middle East for most of history, while the nation-state as we know it today as introduced after the fall of the Ottoman Empire. Tribal identity, though not as strong as it once was, still plays a role in many countries across the region, including Iraq and Libya.

In Jordan, tribalism has created a give-and-take between the state and tribal leaders. For example, the courts often allow tribal leaders to negotiate a desired sentence when members of their tribes are involved in a case. Although the presence of tribes can signify challenges to the state's authority, in the case of Jordan, tribal involvement in these kinds of matters has allowed the state to rely on the legitimacy of tribal leaders to promote stability and peaceful resolution to conflicts.

Voting is also done along tribal lines, although resurgent Islamist political parties, including the Muslim Brotherhood, have also influenced politics in recent years. This poses more of a challenge to the state, because favoritism becomes an issue as tribal identity shapes the way politicians vote and act. A 2014 survey of Jordanians found that many felt politicians responded to their tribal kinsmen more quickly than those outside of their tribe, which undermines the nation's ability to govern as a whole.

Jordan, which has few natural resources and relies on natural gas and oil imports to meet their domestic needs, has the largest refugee population in the world. The country has around 2.8 million refugees living within their borders, which is about one-third of Jordan's non-refugee population. Most refugees live in camps, which receive aid from international organizations and foreign governments. But even so, Jordan's economy is under great strain as more and more refugees enter the country; in 2015 alone, one million Syrians fleeing civil war in their country crossed the border. The country is also home to a large number of Palestinian refugees, many of whom have lived in Jordanian refugee camps for decades.

Lebanon

Bordered by Syria, Israel, and the Mediterranean Sea, Lebanon has a unique political structure designed to maintain balance between the religious groups in the country. The public votes for the parliament every four years, and the parliament then elects a president. Together, the president and parliament appoint a prime minister. The state is organized around confessionalism, a structure that guarantees equitable power sharing between religious groups. The speaker of parliament must be Shia Muslim, the president must be Maronite Christian, and the prime minister must be a Sunni Muslim. The 128-seat parliament is divided equally among Christians and Muslims.

However, that political system has been unable to function in recent years due to a stalemate that has left the country without a president since 2014. Parliament has been unable to agree on someone to appoint for the position, leaving the governing of the country up to the cabinet, where decisions require unanimous approval. The leadership crisis led to protests in summer 2015, when allegations that prominent Sunni politician Saad al-Hariri was profiting from a waste management contract stopped garbage collection across the country. Further exacerbating political and religious tensions in Lebanon has been the influx of nearly 700,000 Syrian refugees in a country of only 4.5 million residents.

Hezbollah, a Shia Islamist militant group, has a stronghold in the south of Lebanon. The group is considered a terrorist organization by Western powers and receives backing from Iran. Hezbollah is outspokenly anti-Israel and launches attacks on the

Bedouins

The Bedouins are an ancient Arab nomadic society, with a population of around twenty-one million spread across the Middle East and North Africa. Bedouins are traditionally animal herders, traveling across the desert with camels, goats, and sheep. In Jordan, they make up around 35 percent of the population, living primarily in the eastern deserts of the country. One tribe, the Bani Hasan, numbers one million, although there are many smaller groups as well. Bedouin culture has adapted to the nation state system by settling to various degrees. While some still travel consistently across the desert, others remain in one place for periods of time before moving on or have created permanent communities. In the past, governments have discriminated against nomadic culture, attempting to force them to abandon their traditional ways of life. In Jordan, however, the king has recognized the importance of Bedouin culture, and the government now works with the Bedouins to ensure they receive education, health care, and housing if they need it. The Bedouins have long maintained some autonomy from governments due in part to their mobility, and their loyalty to their tribe is seen as a threat to central rule.

state from their territory in Lebanon. But Hezbollah is also a political party and routinely wins seats in elections. Due to their presence in government, they are able to use the structure based on compromise to help promote their platform of Islamist governance.

The place of Islam in government has long been a challenge for states in the Middle East and North Africa, and the international community often looks at Islamist parties with fear due to extremist groups like ISIS and al-Qaeda. In some cases, such as in Iraq where Shia leader Muqtada al-Sadr is able to have significant influence outside of the government, states feel religious political leaders pose a threat to their legitimacy. But in the case of Lebanon and others, Islamist groups have proven capable for providing services the state cannot guarantee, particularly in Lebanon where political gridlock means outside organizations have an opportunity to meet those needs. The case of Hezbollah underscores a paradox for Middle Eastern politics: with the state unable to meet the needs of the people, outside groups are able to gain legitimacy by filling that role, which allows them to gain enough support to eventually become part of the state themselves.

Syria

Bordered by Turkey, Israel, Lebanon, Iraq, and the Mediterranean Sea, Syria is an ethnically and religiously diverse country with a rich history. It has also been plagued by conquest, war, and repression. The Arab Socialist Baath Party has dominated politics in Syria since independence in 1946, and although on paper the country has a representative presidential political system, in reality, power has

Bashar al-Assad is the president of Syria. Under his rule, the country has descended into an ongoing civil war.

been centralized in the hands of the ruling Assad family. Through the repression of dissidents and staged elections, the presidency passed from Hafez al-Assad to his son, Bashar al-Assad, in 2000.

Since 2011, Syria has emerged as one of the most urgent and deadly conflicts of the twenty-first century. When protests against President Bashar al-Assad's eleven-year rule began in March 2011, the government offered reforms. But protests continued, and Assad began a violent crackdown that would escalate into a full-scale civil war that, as of 2016, has displaced an estimated 9.5 million people and killed as many as 400,000.

Demonstrations began in the small city of Daraa but quickly spread to cities across the country. Protesters spoke out against economic hardship and lack of freedom, calling for Assad to lift the forty-eight-year state of emergency that had allowed the president to sidestep checks and balances enshrined in the constitution. By May of 2011, however, the government had responded by sending troops to stop demonstrations, and fighting quickly escalated. Although still maintaining control of the capital city, Damascus, Assad's government has carried out extensive bombing in cities like Aleppo and Homs, and has been accused of carrying out chemical weapons attacks against civilians.

The Syrian civil war has given rise to widespread instability. ISIS, or the Islamic State, has carved out a stronghold in Syria and northern Iraq, using the Syrian city of Raqqa as their base of operations. The group, a former al-Qaeda branch that split with the organization and has since drawn hundreds of foreign fighters to Syria, as well as pledges of allegiance from other terrorist organizations around the world, made headlines with their ideology of hatred and use of extreme violence.

The large number of refugees driven from Syria has also caused a global crisis, straining local governments and prompting many to try to cross the Mediterranean or through Turkey to get to Europe. The United Nations estimates that around three million refugees have fled to neighboring countries, many of which already have a high number of refugees from Palestine and other countries. Other refugees have turned to human smugglers, who are paid large sums of money by refugees to get them to safety in Europe. But they often rely on unsafe routes and unreliable modes of transportation. Small rafts that cannot cross the Mediterranean have disappeared with numerous passengers, while many have died crossing land due to poor ventilation in the backs of trucks and other vehicles. An estimated 6.5 million are displaced within Syria, many of whom require humanitarian assistance and medical attention but are isolated due to ongoing fighting.

Regional Relations

For most of the twentieth century, relations between states in the Levant were dominated by conflict. Israel went to war multiple times with neighboring states, beginning soon after Israel declared independence in 1948. In the Six-Day War of 1976, Israel fought Syria, Egypt, and Jordan, as well as troops from North African and Gulf states, and expanded their territory to include the Sinai Peninsula, the Golan Heights, the Gaza Strip, and the West Bank. Egypt (in 1978) and Jordan (in 1994) signed formal peace treaties with Israel that allowed their governments to cooperate on security matters and the sharing of resources.

While Jordan, Egypt, and Israel have established an arrangement that allows for cooperation, Syria and Lebanon have close ties to Iran. The Iranian government has supported the Shia Assad regime in the Syrian civil war, and Hezbollah acts as an Iranian proxy in Lebanon. This relationship has caused conflict in the region, with Iran providing training and funding that has helped Hezbollah carry out attacks on Israel. Hezbollah has also provided support to the Assad regime, which has drawn criticism from the Lebanese public.

Non-State Actors in the Levant

Today, the largest challenge to stability in the Levant and state relations is non-state actors, including groups like Hamas in the

Gaza Strip and Hezbollah in Lebanon. These groups, unlike groups like al-Qaeda that do not pursue traditional political control, disrupt the established nation-state system by holding considerable influence in areas where they are active. Hamas, recognized as a terrorist organization in the West, rules the Gaza Strip, from which they engage in frequent conflict with Israeli forces. As discussed, Hezbollah has become part of the political system and has launched regular attacks on Israel from their territory. The Muslim Brotherhood, a political and military party founded in Egypt and marginalized from power, is also active in Jordan and Lebanon.

Syria's instability makes it a hotbed for extremist, non-state activity, a significant concern among leadership around the world. In 2013, an offshoot branch of al-Qaeda in Iraq sought refuge in Syria during the civil war there and became ISIS. The group, led by Abu Bakr al-Baghdadi, captured cities and territory across southern Syria and northern Iraq throughout 2014, setting up their de facto capital in the Syrian city of Raqqa. Cultish and social-media savvy, ISIS follows a Wahhabi strain of ultra-conservative Sunni Islam that is rooted in violence and exclusion. Their ideology, though based in an extreme interpretation of Islam, has been denounced by Muslim leaders worldwide, and Muslims have been among their many victims.

Although since then airstrikes and cooperative efforts between regional and international states has contained ISIS's territorial growth, the group has become a magnet for foreign fighters. Thousands of Jordanians have crossed into Syria to join the group, and Europe has struggled to stem the flow of fighters traveling

Khaled Meshaal is the leader of Hamas in the Gaza Strip. The group has controlled the Gaza Strip since 2007.

to the region. These fighters pose a threat to regional states and the international community, as ISIS has encouraged fighters to plan attacks in their own countries. This decentralized mode of operation has allowed for disparate groups and individuals around the world to pledge allegiance to the group without ever traveling to the region, allowing their network to expand even as their territory shrinks.

But ISIS has also brought the Middle East and North Africa together, as all states work to find a way to eradicate the threat. Talks to find a solution to the crisis in Syria, which has allowed groups like ISIS to proliferate due to the lack of governance in the country, are ongoing, and military cooperation between regional states and the international community have targeted ISIS territory.

Markets like this one in Fez, Morocco, are common across the Middle East.

4

Modern-Day Geography, Government, and Conflict in North Africa

North Africa, which includes Libya, Algeria, Morocco, and Tunisia, makes up the northern border of the African continent. All four countries have coasts along the Mediterranean Sea, and Morocco borders the Atlantic. To the south, North Africa borders Mauritania, Mali, Niger, Chad, and Sudan, which is sometimes considered part of North Africa due to the country's strong Islamic and Arab population. In this book, Sudan is not considered part of North Africa. The Islamic Empire once controlled these North African countries and, as a result, they have a great deal in common with the culture and religion of the Middle East.

Algeria

Once a French colony, Algeria borders Tunisia, Libya, Morocco, and the Mediterranean Sea. The country gained independence in 1962. But by the late 1980s, escalating rivalry between political factions led to a civil war, which lasted until 1999. That year, Abdelaziz Bouteflika won a presidential election that all other candidates dropped out of at the last minute, guaranteeing him and his military backers the high office. Bouteflika has remained in office ever since, despite health issues and infrequent public appearances.

Under the Algerian constitution, both the president and one half of the parliament are elected by popular vote, while the other half of the parliament is voted for by electoral representatives in a style similar to the United States's electoral college. The president appoints a prime minister from the party with the majority of parliamentary seats. But while multiparty politics have been a part of Algeria's system for decades, power remains tightly held by Bouteflika. Even recent reforms to the constitution, passed in 2016, do not take power away from Bouteflika; in fact, a new term limit for the presidency doesn't apply to him at all, and he will be allowed to run for a fifth term when his current fourth term ends in 2019.

Algeria is known as a police state, in which the police force and military play a prominent role in maintaining the status

Abdelaziz Bouteflika has ruled Algeria since 1999. He is supported by the military, and his party controls politics in Algeria.

quo. Bouteflika, who was the military-backed candidate in the 1999 election, has centralized control of the intelligence services under his administration, and high-ranking military officials have extensive freedoms. Bouteflika's National Liberation Front party dominates all politics in the country.

Despite these undemocratic trends, Algeria does have something that some other states in the Middle East and North Africa do not have: stability. Protests against authoritarianism have not rattled the state's power, and Algeria has been aggressive in their attempts to combat extremism both within their own borders and in cooperation with international forces in nearby states, such as Mali.

Libya

Once an Italian colony, Libya borders Tunisia, Algeria, and Egypt. The country emerged from the colonial era as a dictatorship under Colonel Muammar Qaddafi. Qaddafi, sometimes spelled "Gaddafi" or "Kadafi," led a military coup against King Idris in 1969, overthrowing the monarchy and installing himself as Libya's ruler. Qaddafi ruled Libya until 2011, when popular protests forced him from office. Since then, however, militias have struggled to fill the power vacuum Qaddafi left behind, and Libya has fallen into an ongoing civil crisis.

In 2014, a constitutional commission was elected to work on a draft of the Libyan constitution. A second draft of the document, released by the group in February 2016, is called the Constitutional Drafting Assembly. The draft includes several features aimed at restoring peace and addressing longstanding concerns, including popular support for decentralizing the government. Under Qaddafi, many felt that power was too centralized in the capital city of Tripoli and, as a result, wealth and opportunity were not equally shared across the country. To help this, the constitution names three capitals: Tripoli, Benghazi, and Sabha. These cities would divide federal duties and offices. But the country has a long way to go before peace is restored.

Since 2011, Libya has effectively been split into two separate zones, with a third developing in the north around the city of Sirte, where ISIS has set up a stronghold. In the east, the elected Tobruk government is in power, which is recognized by the international community as the official government of the country. In the

Muammar Qaddafi was forced from office by protests in 2011. Since then, Libya has fallen into civil war.

west, the Muslim Brotherhood-led Islamist General National Congress holds the capital city of Tripoli. A ceasefire brokered by the United Nations has allowed for the reconciliation process to begin under a unity government, called the Government of National Accord.

But Libya has a long history of tribalism, and when Qaddafi's forces cracked down on protesters, militias began forming along tribal lines. Under Qaddafi, who was a strong supporter of Arab nationalism, ethnic and culturally distinct groups within Libya suffered persecution and discrimination. Now, those groups are fighting to ensure that they have a voice in the new government. Within those two dominant zones, tribes with various ethnic allegiances control local areas.

These pockets of authority undermine the government's ability to unify and rule. Just as in Syria, the lack of structure has created openings for non-state actors, such as ISIS, to take territory and set up their own areas of control. Neighboring states now fear that Libya, which is oil-rich and has access to a wide coastline that connects it to the rest of the Mediterranean, could become a haven for extremists. A large number of Libyans are now fleeing their country to escape violence and poor living conditions.

Morocco

Controlled by the French until 1956, Morocco sits in the northwestern corner of Africa. The constitution was amended via referendum numerous times throughout the twentieth century and, more recently, the monarch, King Mohammed, initiated reforms after public protests demanded democracy.

Morocco is a constitutional monarchy with a bicameral parliament. The 325-member Assembly of Representatives, the lower house of parliament, is elected by popular vote, and elections include 30 seats reserved for women. The upper house, or the 270-member Assembly of Councillors, is elected by a combination of elites, including local councils. In the 2011 elections, fifteen parties won seats in parliament, with almost twice that on the ballot.

Within the multiparty system, the Islamist Justice and Development Party (JDP) is the strongest force outside of the monarchy. The king tasked the group's leader, Abdelilah Benkirane, to form a coalition government in 2012 as prime minister. Moderate and popular, Benkirane and his party have worked to combat corruption in the government, and the king has allowed for a power-sharing arrangement to develop. This has opened up space for pluralism, or the existence of more than one group to share authority in the government.

But many feel the political system remains too closed off, with too much power resting in the king's hands. The Justice and Development Party is not the only Islamist party in the country, but it is the only one with a significant following that isn't banned. JPD is seen as being willing to compromise and work with the king rather than challenge his authority, which ultimately serves to strengthen the king's power. International human rights groups have also found that the government continues to crack down on the media and individuals who criticize the king, an illegal act under Moroccan law.

In addition to the country of Morocco, the government also controls the Western Sahara, a coastal area once held by the Spanish and declared an independent country by the indigenous Sahrawi people in 1976. Although an internationally brokered ceasefire ended decades of conflict in the area, Morocco still occupies most of the territory. The unrecognized Saharawi Republic, meanwhile, holds a small area in the east and operates refugee camps in Algeria. Morocco's continued occupation of Western Sahara has led to increased tensions with its neighbor, Algeria. The border between the two countries has been closed since 1994.

Tunisia

A former French protectorate, Tunisia borders Algeria and Libya, as well as the Mediterranean Sea. General Zine al-Abidine Ben Ali controlled the country from 1987 to 2011, when the Arab Spring began there and forced Ben Ali into exile.

The Arab Spring, a wave of protests that swept across the Middle East and radically reshaped the understanding of power in the region, started in December 2010 in the Tunisian city of Ben Arous. A fruit vendor named Mohamed Bouazizi, who was often harassed and extorted by local authorities, had his goods taken from him by police. When he was unable to get them back,

Saharawi Republic

Located to the south of Morocco along the Atlantic coastline, the Western Sahara is a disputed territory divided between occupying Morocco and the Saharawi Republic. The Saharawi Republic, declared in 1976 by the indigenous Saharawi people, is recognized by the African Union and some states, but is not recognized by the United Nations. Morocco, Algeria, and Mauritania fought for decades over rightful claim to this land, and the Polisario Front, an independence movement, opposed all their claims. Although an internationally brokered ceasefire ended decades of conflict in the area, Morocco still occupies most of the territory. The Saharawi Republic, meanwhile, holds a small area in the east and operates refugee camps in Algeria. The United Nations Security Council established the Mission for the Referendum in Western Sahara to give the Saharawi people the chance to decide how they want to be governed, but under the terms of the ceasefire Morocco must agree to when and how the referendum will be carried out. So far Morocco has not done so, in part because of their economic control of the area, which they will lose if the area becomes an independent state.

Bouazizi took to the middle of a busy street and set himself on fire in protest. His death lead to widespread protests across the county, with demonstrators decrying high unemployment, corruption, lack of democracy, and violations of human rights. A month later, Ben Ali resigned and left the country.

Tunisia was the first of multiple countries that experienced political change thanks to popular protests that year, and many were watching closely to see how the story unfolded next. Although for a time it seemed Tunisia might have fallen to infighting as a new government was formed, the country was able to pull through years of turmoil with relative stability. The Tunisian National Dialogue Quartet, a group of four organizations that received the 2015 Nobel Peace Prize in recognition for their efforts, tirelessly worked to mediate between the many factions within the government, paving the way for a smooth transition to democracy.

Under the 2014 constitution, Tunisia's president is elected by popular vote to a five-year term. The president, who must be Muslim to run for office, appoints the prime minister and a cabinet. The parliament, or the Assembly of the Representatives of the People, is also elected by direct vote, with the first elections held in late 2014. The constitution outlines a target of gender equality in elected bodies, which is the first time such a commitment has been made in North Africa or the Middle East.

Regional Relations

North Africa is uniquely placed as the cultural crossroads between Africa and the Middle East. All North African states are part

The National Dialogue Quartet was awarded the Nobel Peace Prize in 2015 for their work in post-revolution Tunisia.

of the African Union, with the exception of Morocco, which left the organization after the African Union recognized the Saharawi Republic.

Although Tunisia and Egypt have established strong relations after their 2011 revolutions, relations in the region are dominated by concern over extremism from Libya. Morocco and Algeria have not had diplomatic relations since the 1963 Sand War in the Western Sahara and have had a closed border since 1994.

More broadly, North African states have strong ties to the Middle East, particularly Tunisia. Tunisia has fostered strong relations with most Middle Eastern countries, through economic agreements and resource sharing projects. Libya, long erratic under Qaddafi, has had tense relations with most states in the region, and today the continued unrest there is overshadowed by the Syrian civil war but remains a significant concern.

All North African states, with the exception of Libya, are full members of the Union of the Mediterranean. Formed in 2008, the organization brings together all European Union States, the Arab League, and states along the Mediterranean to facilitate cooperation. Libya is an observer state and has expressed interest in joining the organization.

Religion and Politics

In the West, the separation of church and state is a key value in most countries. But the role of religion in the politics of the Middle East and North Africa is far more complex. Islam, the dominant religion of the region, developed as both a faith and a political system at the same time as the Islamic empire spread. As a result, the teachings of Islam include guidelines for governance, and religious organizations and clerics play an important role in meeting the needs of the public. This can include charity work or direct roles in the government.

Refugee camps in Algeria are home to thousands of Sahrawi people, who once lived in the disputed Western Sahara.

In North Africa, Islamic political parties have long been the most vocal opponents of the political establishment, and many have shifted towards a pro-democracy stance in response to authoritarianism. In many cases, Islamic parties are better organized than other possible opposition parties and are seen as less corrupt due to their ties to faith. After the Arab Spring, they were best placed to fill the resulting power vacuums, particularly in states where healthy debate and pluralism were restricted by dictators.

Although Iran is the only true **theocracy** in the region, almost all states in the Middle East and North Africa include elements of religiosity in their political framework. In North Africa, this can take many forms. In some cases, the monarch serves as a religious leader, such as the king of Morocco's legitimacy coming in part from his being *sayyid*, or descended from the Prophet Muhammad. In others, Islam is recognized as the state religion, or sharia serves as the basis of law, as it does in Algeria and Egypt. In Tunisia, all candidates for president are required to be Muslim.

Political Islam differs from extremism, as seen in groups like al-Qaeda and ISIS. Political Islamic parties most often want to function within the established government through democratic elections, while extremist groups use terrorism to undermine the power structure. But in states where authoritarian leadership wants to exclude Islamist parties, they often rely on fear of extremism to justify cracking down on these groups. Most violent Islamist groups draw inspiration from Salafist teachings, which are closely linked with the Wahhabi tradition in Saudi Arabia.

Supreme Leader Ayatollah Ali Khamenei is the most powerful man in Iran, with final say on all matters of the state.

5

Important Figures in Geography, Government, and Conflict Across the Middle East

The Middle East and North Africa have long been shaped by those who hold power in the region, and many leaders can remain in power for decades. This chapter examines important figures in the region and their influence on their countries today.

The Gulf Region

Bahrain

Ghada Jamshir has been a long-time advocate of women's rights in Bahrain and has petitioned for reform in sharia courts in the country. Jamshir argues that jurisdiction over family and women's issues should be overseen by civil courts instead of sharia courts and oversees the Women's Petition Committee to change Bahrain's laws. Because of her outspokenness on Bahrain's laws, she has run into trouble in Bahrain and has claimed the government, headed by Shaikh Hamad ibn Isa Al Khalifa, has spied on her and sent people to bribe and blackmail her.

Iran

Supreme Leader Ayatollah Ali Khamenei is the most powerful man in Iran and is the second person to hold the title of Supreme Leader. He became the political and religious authority of Iran in 1989, after Ayatollah Ruhollah Khomeini, the first Supreme Leader and the leader of the Islamic Revolution, passed away. The Supreme Leader, who is chosen by the elected Assembly of Experts, is tasked with ensuring the country follows Islamic teachings and serving as the ultimate guide for Iran. As Supreme Leader, Khamenei has ultimate control over everything that happens in the country, including all international affairs and domestic policies. He also controls the military. Khamenei, who does not give interviews to Western media and has not left Iran since serving as president in the 1980s, is seen as conservative and opposed to reform, but he must approve all significant policy changes in Iran. This includes the nuclear deal that ended the decade-long Iranian nuclear crisis. The president, elected every four years, is allowed varying levels of freedom to pursue policies of his choice, but Khamenei has been known to play a more active role when he does not agree with the direction in which Iran is heading and is a constant presence in the political culture.

Iraq

In post-Saddam Hussein Iraq, Muqtada al-Sadr has established himself as one of the core authorities in the country. Al-Sadr, a Shia cleric and political leader, once led the Mahdi Army against United States-led coalition forces. Today, he is leading the charge to reform Iraq's dysfunctional political system, with his supporters storming the so-called Green Zone around the nation's capital. Although he doesn't hold office, al-Sadr is the spiritual and de facto leader of his own political movement, which includes the al-Ahrar bloc of Iraq's parliament. Like Hassan Nasrallah in Lebanon, the loyalty of his followers and their positions of power are enough for al-Sadr to hold significant influence. It may be unclear to many what his intentions are—whether it's truly reforming Iraq's government or placing one of his allies in higher office—but it is clear that he has the tools to achieve his goals.

Kuwait

Sabah Al-Sabah has been emir of Kuwait and commander of the Kuwaiti military since 2006. During his reign he has pursued some reforms, such as appointing the emirate's first female minister and

The President

In this film, made by Iranian filmmaker Mohsen Makhmalbaf, the dictator of an unnamed country is faced with widespread protests that threaten his regime. After sending his family to safety, he and his young grandson are forced to journey through the hostile country disguised as gypsies. Outside of the safety of the palace and unprotected by the political establishment, the dictator confronts the struggles of his people, including poverty and hunger. Made in 2014, *The President* came on the heels of protests across the region, and explores the humanity of both the protesters and those who become dictators. Makhmalbaf made the details of the film's setting particularly vague so that the audience could see any country and any leader in it, from modern-day Libya to Iran in 1979. His film asks whether anyone, even leaders who are hated, is fully bad and whether those who oppose these leaders are fully good, questions that are increasingly important in places like Syria, where the al-Assad regime is locked in conflict with groups that are equally brutal and authoritarian. The film also underlines the need for cultural changes, as well as political changes, for democracy to thrive.

promoting religious tolerance in schools. Al-Sabah also passed a law that guarantees media freedom in Kuwait, one of the strongest such laws in the Middle East.

Oman

Sultan Qaboos deposed his father in 1970 and took the throne of Oman. His reign has focused on modernization, economic reforms, and increased spending in education and health care. However, he continues to rule by decree and often clamps down on any dissenters of his rule. In fact, Sultan Qaboos's power is so absolute that his birthday, November 18, is celebrated as a national holiday in Oman.

Qatar

Sheikha bint Ahmed al-Mahmoud became Qatar's first female cabinet minister in 2003 when she was named minister of education. She paved the way for other female ministers in Qatar, including Dr. Hessa Al Jaber, named minister of communication and information technology in 2013, and Sheikha Ghalia bint Mohammad bin Hamad al-Thani, a member of the ruling family who was named minister of health in 2008. In 2016, Dr. Hanan Mohamed Al Kuwari was the most recent woman to be named to Qatar's cabinet as minister of health.

Saudi Arabia

The House of Saud refers to the Saudi royal family, the only family to rule Saudi Arabia. The family is extremely large, and almost all members of the family are given roles in the government. The king, Salman Al Saud, is the head of government and of the family, and he names members of his family to positions ranging from cabinet posts to provincial governorships. This high level of presence in the government helps the House of Saud maintain power, as no opposition leaders have been able to gain a significant leadership position. A hereditary absolute monarchy, power in Saudi Arabia lies solely with the ruling family. As a result, they are one of the most powerful families in the Middle East, ruling over a large, wealthy country with significant influence among their neighbors.

United Arab Emirates

The Al Nahyan family rules over the emirate of Abu Dhabi and has ruled over this territory since the eighteenth century. Khalifa ibn Zayid al-Nahyan is the president of the UAE in addition to being the ruler of Abu Dhabi, and his son, Mohammed ibn Zayid al-Nahyan is the heir apparent to the throne. The al-Nahyan family is believed to be worth over $150 billion dollars.

Yemen

Ali Abdullah Saleh was president of Yemen from 1990 until 2012. He was forced to step down following a wave of protests and discontent with his presidency. After fleeing Yemen and handing over power to his deputy Abd Rabbuh Mansur Hadi, Saleh became allied with Shia Houthi rebels who took over the Yemen government in 2014, which caused Hadi to flee. The civil war is ongoing at the time of this writing.

The Levant Region

Egypt

Abdel Fattah al-Sisi became the leader of Egypt after the 2013 military coup against former president Mohammed Morsi, the first president after the 2011 revolution unseated Hosni Mubarak. Al-Sisi went on to win the presidential election held in 2014 with over 93 percent of the vote, standing against just one other candidate. His time in office has been marked by a return

Abdel Fattah al-Sisi became president of Egypt in 2014, following a coup against Mohammed Morsi.

to the violent suppression of protesters seen under Mubarak, and political power has been centralized in his hands. Al-Sisi has also favored the army, awarding them building contracts that cannot be appealed under Egyptian law. Under him, detention limits have been lifted, allowing dissidents to be held in prison indefinitely without charges.

Israel

Benjamin Netanyahu has been prime minister of Israel since 2002 and is the leader of the conservative Likud Party. Prior to his political career, he was a member of the Israeli Defense Forces, fighting in numerous operations and conflicts, including the 1973 Yom Kippur War. He was also the Israeli United Nations ambassador from 1984 to 1988, and he first served as Israel's prime minister from 1996 to 1999. Netanyahu is known as being hawkish and nationalist and has positioned himself in direct opposition to Iran. Under his leadership, peace negotiations between the Palestinian and Israeli governments have stalled, and the building of settlements in the West Bank has continued despite calls from the United Nations for them to stop. When Netanyahu completes his current term, he will be the longest-serving prime minister in the history of Israel, having guided the country for over a decade.

Jordan

King of the Hashemite Kingdom of Jordan, Abdullah II succeeded his father in 1999. The throne almost was not passed to him; his father named Abdullah heir just days before his death. Since

Benjamin Netanyahu is on track to be the longest-serving prime minister in Israeli history.

becoming king, Abdullah has worked closely with world and regional powers on issues such a combatting extremism, refugee rights, and the Israeli-Palestinian conflict. He has also moved to make Jordan more democratic, embrace religious diversity, empower political parties, and liberalize the strained Jordanian economy. His wife, Queen Rania, has also taken a prominent role in advancing children's rights and education, as well as being active on social media and in representing Jordan in popular culture.

Lebanon

Hassan Nasrallah has been leader of Lebanon's Hezbollah since 1992, leading the group through numerous conflicts with Israel and to political influence within Lebanon. The current political crisis gripping the country, which has not had a president since 2014, has allowed Hezbollah to further assert power, making Nasrallah even more powerful than he once was. Although he does not hold office himself, he is popular among the Lebanese public and is supported by Iran, and his place outside of the establishment allows him to stay above politics while playing an active role in them. Like Muqtada al-Sadr in Iraq, Nasrallah has effectively established himself as an alternative leader with significant influence.

Palestine

Chairman of the Palestinian Liberation Organization since 2004 and the President of Palestine since 2005, Mahmoud Abbas is the leader of what the international community recognizes as the Palestinian government. He is responsible for governing the West Bank and for taking part in negotiations between Palestine and Israel. Originally elected for a five-year presidential term, Abbas extended his term of office due to infighting among Palestinian leadership, a decision that caused a break with Hamas in the Gaza Strip. Abbas, who supports a peaceful solution to the ongoing Israeli-Palestinian conflict, has struggled to control extremist groups that operate within the West Bank, and many believe his political party, Fatah, is corrupt. His working relationship with Israel, though strained, has also drawn criticism

Hassan Nasrallah is the leader of Hezbollah in Lebanon, where he has amassed significant influence and power.

from those who feel a more aggressive approach is needed to bring an end to the conflict.

Syria

Bashar al-Assad is the President of Syria, having taken office after the death of his father, Hafez al-Assad, in 2000. Although he ran for office every seven years, Assad has only run against other candidates once, and then only against candidates sanctioned by the state. As a result, he receives upwards of 85 percent of the vote. Under Assad, the Syrian civil war has torn the country apart, resulting in millions of refugees and unknown numbers of casualties. The country has become a haven for groups like ISIS, and today Assad controls only the area immediately surrounding the capital of Damascus, although his forces carry out airstrikes in cities around the country. Assad has refused to step down from office and, as the situation has deteriorated, many are concerned that allowing him to remain in office is the only way to move toward ending the conflict. Negotiations between the international community, Syrian opposition groups, and the Syrian government are ongoing as of the time of this writing.

North Africa

Algeria

Louisa Hanoune is the head of the country's Worker's Party, a left-wing political party that focuses on increasing support for trade union and labor justice. Prior to 1988, political parties other than the leading party were illegal in Algeria, and Hanoune was

Louise Hanoune leads Algeria's Worker's Party, a leftist party, and was the first woman to run for president in the region.

jailed several times for her political activism. In 2004, she became the first woman in the Middle East or North Africa to ever run for president. She ran again in 2009 and 2014. In 2014, Hanoune came in fourth place, although she received less than 2 percent of the Algerian vote.

Libya

Khalifa Haftar leads the Libyan National Army and has been a huge influence in the continued Libyan Civil War. Haftar served as a general under Qaddafi before trying to overthrow him in the late 1980s. He fled to the United States, where he stayed for many years. When the Libyan Civil War began in 2011, Haftar helped to lead the opposition forces that would overthrow the Libyan president. He has continued to lead the National Army against Islamist forces in the country and other opposing factions.

Morocco

Since 2012, Bassima Hakkaoui has been Minister of Solidary, Women, Family, and Social Development in the cabinet of the Moroccan prime minister, Abdelilah Benkirane. She has also been elected to the House of Representatives twice, in 2007 and 2011. In 2016, Hakkaoui announced a new draft of an anti-sexual

Beji Caid Essebsi is the first democratically elected president of post-revolution Tunisia.

harassment law that would impose more stringent punishments for those who commit sexual crimes against women. However, Hakkaoui has also been criticized by Moroccan women who feel she hasn't done enough to improve women's situation in Morocco.

Tunisia

Elected president of Tunisia in 2014, Beji Caid Essebsi is the country's first democratically elected president. Prior to the revolution, he was an ally of General Ben Ali, and became interim prime minister when Ben Ali's appointee stepped down in 2011. After leaving the position of prime minister later that year, he founded a secular political party, called Nida Tounes, which went on to win a majority of seats in the country's first elections in 2014. As president, Essebsi has vowed to represent and work for all citizens of Tunisia, marking a new day in Tunisian politics after decades of dictatorship.

Chronology

1916	The Great Arab Revolt against Ottoman rule begins.
1918–1920	The collapse of the Ottoman Empire leaves most Arab countries under European control.
1932	The Kingdom of Saudi Arabia is unified and declared.
1948	Israel declares independence; the first Arab-Israeli War begins.
1953	CIA's Operation Ajax overthrows the first democratically elected government in Iran.
1956	Crisis erupts in Egypt over nationalization of the Suez Canal.
1967	The Six-Day War between Arab states and Israel; Israel expands held territories
1979	The Islamic Revolution in Iran unseats the monarchy and establishes an Islamic Republic.
1980–1988	The Iran-Iraq War is fought.
1991	Iraq invades Kuwait; US-led first Gulf War in Iraq begins.

1991–1999	The Algerian civil war is fought.
2003	The US-led invasion of Iraq unseats Iraqi leader Saddam Hussein.
2010–2011	Arab Spring protests unseat leaders in Tunisia, Egypt, and Libya; reforms are made in other regional states.
2011	The Syrian civil war begins.
2015	The Yemeni civil war begins.

Map of the Region

Map of the Region

Glossary

Arab Spring A series of uprisings across the Middle East that began in 2011 in Tunisia and spread throughout the Arab world, in some cases spurring civil wars.

authoritarian A system of government in which one person or group has central power and political freedom is limited.

bey The governor of a district in the Ottoman Empire; sometimes used as a courtesy title today.

caliphate An area governed by a caliph, considered the religious successor to the Prophet Muhammad.

cleric A religious leader, especially Christian or Muslim.

federation A group of states that have some autonomy, but come together to form a union under a central government.

jurisprudence A legal system, or the philosophy behind a country's laws.

Kurds An ethnic group of people in the Middle East who are mainly Muslim and speak Kurdish; they are not Arab.

martial law When a government temporarily does away with civil law and the military controls the country.

nationalization The running of certain industries or companies by the state, with profits going to the government.

nomads Societies that travel consistently and do not have a permanent settlement.

non-state actors Groups that function outside of the government but still have considerable influence or power.

partition To divide something, such as land, into smaller parts.

populist A political view considered more concerned with the rights and good of the people than with elites. A populist is someone seen as appealing to the general public.

protectorates States that come under the control of other countries but retain their own government.

provincial Describes regions beyond the capital city, meaning rural areas and places distant from the power center.

sanction A penalty that is put in place to bring about change through economic pressure; sanctions make it illegal for other countries or organizations to do business with the penalized country or organization.

sects The branches of larger religious traditions, such as Shia and Sunni Islam.

sharia Islamic law, taken from the teachings of the Prophet Muhammad.

Silk Road Ancient trade routes that connected China to the Mediterranean Sea.

sovereign Describes a nation that fully controls its own government, affairs, and borders.

theocracy A system of government in which the political system is controlled by religious leaders and with religious legitimacy.

Further Information

Books

Dabashi, Hamid. *The Arab Spring: The End of Postcolonialism*. New York: Zed Books, 2012.

Danahar, Paul. *The New Middle East: The World After the Arab Spring*. London, UK: Bloomsbury, 2015.

Fraihat, Ibrahimi. *Unfinished Revolutions: Yemen, Libya, and Tunisia after the Arab Spring*. New Haven, CT: Yale University Press, 2016.

Lewis, Bernard. *The Middle East*. New York: Simon & Schuster, 1995.

Majd, Hooman. *The Ayatollah's Democracy*. New York: W.W. Norton & Co, 2010.

Websites

The Council on Foreign Relations

http://www.cfr.org

The official website for an organization that researches and publishes work on major international affairs issues. The site includes pages dedicated to specific countries, issues, and important figures, which provide key historical context and expert analysis.

The Middle East Institute

http://www.mei.edu

The official website for a nonprofit organization dedicated to researching and providing analysis of breaking news in the Middle East and surrounding countries. The Middle East Institute publishes works on economics, politics, conflict, and other issues.

The United Nations: The Middle East

http://www.un.org/en/sections/where-we-work/middle-east

The United Nations conducts projects and research on conditions in the Middle East and North Africa and publishes information about key issues in the region. The organization has a high level of access to countries other groups are not able to observe or enter, and it has a comprehensive backlog of UN resolutions and decisions passed regarding the region.

Bibliography

Axworthy, Michael. *Revolutionary Iran: A History of the Islamic Republic*. Oxford, UK: Oxford University Press, 2013.

Filiu, Jean-Pierre. *The Arab Revolution: Ten Lessons from the Democratic Uprising*. Oxford, UK: Oxford University Press, 2011.

Fromkin, David. *A Peace to End All Peace: The Fall of the Ottoman Empire and the Creation of the Modern Middle East*. New York: Henry Holt and Co, 1989.

Gasiorowski, Mark, David Long, and Bernard Reich eds. *The Government and Politics of the Middle East and North Africa*. Boulder, CO: Perseus, 2014.

Gerges, Fawaz A. *ISIS: A History*. Princeton, NJ: Princeton University Press, 2016.

Haass, Richard N. "The New Middle East." *Foreign Affairs* (2006). https://www.foreignaffairs.com/articles/middle-east/2006-11-01/new-middle-east.

House, Karen Elliott. *On Saudi Arabia: Its People, Past, Religion, Fault Lines—and Future*. New York: Random House, 2012.

Lippman, Thomas W. *Saudi Arabia on the Edge*. New York: Council on Foreign Relations, 2012.

Mansfield, Peter. *A History of the Middle East*. New York: Penguin, 2013.

Osman, Tarek. *Egypt on the Brink: From Nasser to the Muslim Brotherhood*. New Haven, CT: Yale University Press, 2013.

Rose, Gideon. "The Post-American Middle East." *Foreign Affairs* (2015). https://www.foreignaffairs.com/articles/middle-east/2015-10-20/post-american-middle-east.

Staff of *The Economist*. "Unity, up to a point." *The Economist* (April 2016). http://www.economist.com/news/middle-east-and-africa/21696514-arrival-new-government-brings-hope-war-ravaged-libya-unity-up.

Worth, Robert F. *A Rage for Order: The Middle East in Turmoil, from Tahrir Square to ISIS*. New York: Farrar, Strauss and Giroux, 2016.

Index

Page numbers in **boldface** are illustrations. Entries in **boldface** are glossary terms.

Ahmadinejad, Mahmoud, 37–39
Algeria, 29, 72–73, 96–97
al-Qaeda, 9, 19, 21, 43, 49, 59, 64, 66, 68
Arab Spring protests, 23, 32–33, 36, 43, 46–48, **55**, 77, 82
authoritarian, 5, 8, 15, 20, 33, 73, 82, 83, 88

Bahrain, 12, 35, 44, 46, 51, 86
bey, 32, 33
British **partition** plan, 14

caliphate, 6
cleric, 13, 15, 36, 37, 39, 51, 81, 87

Egypt, 21–23, 54–56, 91–92

federation, 20

Gulf Cooperation Council (GCC), 46–47, 48, 49

Hamas, 27, 37, 57–58, 67–68, 94
Hezbollah, 26, 62–64, 67, 68, 94

Iran, 13–15, 36–39, 86–87
Iraq, 15–16, 39–42, 87
Iraqi **Kurds**, 41
ISIS, 9, 40, 42, 49, 64, 66, 68–69, 74, 83
Islam, 19, 81–83
Israel and Palestine, 7, 23–24, 56–59, 67, 92

Jordan, 24–26, 59–61, 92–93
jurisprudence, 36

Khomeini, Ayatollah Ruhollah, 13–14, **14**, 86
Kurds, 41
Kuwait, 16–17, 87–89

Lamine Bey, 33
Lebanon, 26, 62–64, 64, 94
Libya, 29–31, 74–75, 97–98

martial law, 17
Morocco, 31–32, 76–77, 98–99
Mubarak, Hosni, 23, 54–55, 91–92
Muslim Brotherhood, 28, 56, 59, 61, 68, 75

nationalization, 31
Netanyahu, Benjamin, **57**, 92, **93**
nomadic tradition/**nomads**, 14, 63
non-state actors, 9, 59, 67–69, 75
North Africa, 5, 8–9, 29, 71, 79-81

Oman, 17–18, 46, 89
Ottoman Empire, 7–8, 11, 18

Palestine, 27, 94
partition plan, British, 14
politics, and religion, 81–82
populism/populist figure, 13
protectorates, 5, 31
provincial governorships/relationships, 15, 90

Qaboos, Sultan, 17–18, 89

Qaddafi, Muammar, 31, 74–75, **75**, 81, 98
Qatar, 18, 89

religion, politics and, 81–83

Saharawi Republic, 77, 78, 80
sanctions, 38–39
Saudi Arabia, 19–20, 42–44, 49, 89–90
sects, 21, 53
sharia law, 15, 36, 43, 81
Silk Road, 6
sovereign state, 27
Syria, 28, 64–67, 96

theocracies/theocracy, 8, 82
Tunisia, 32–33, 77–79, 99

United Arab Emirates (UAE), 20, 45, 90

Wahhabism, 19–20, 43, 68, 83
World War I/II, 11, 15, 24, 26, 28, 29, 32

Yemen, 20–21, 48–49, 90

About the Author

Bridey Heing is a writer and book critic based in Washington, DC. She holds degrees in Political Science and International Affairs from DePaul University and Washington University in Saint Louis, Missouri. Her areas of focus are comparative politics and Iranian politics. Her master's thesis explores the evolution of populist politics and democracy in Iran since 1900. She has written about Iranian affairs, women's rights, and art and politics for publications like *The Economist*, *Hyperallergic*, and *The Establishment*. She also writes about literature and film. She enjoys traveling, reading, and exploring Washington, DC's many museums.